Artists in Their World

Paul Klee

Jill A. Laidlaw

W

FRANKLIN WATTS
LONDON•SYDNEY

For Robin Eden

This edition 2005

First published in 2002 by
Franklin Watts, 338 Euston Road
London NW1 3BH

Franklin Watts Australia
Hachette Children's Books
Level 17/207 Kent St
Sydney NSW 2000

© Franklin Watts 2002

Series Editor: Adrian Cole
Series Designer: Mo Choy
Art Director: Jonathan Hair
Picture Researcher: Diana Morris

A CIP catalogue record for this book
is available from the British Library.

ISBN 0 7496 6628 5

Dewey Classification Number 759.9494

Printed in China

Acknowledgements

AKG London: fr cover br, 8, 10t, 16b, 20t, 22t, 23t, 23b, 26t, 28t, 28b, 29t © DACS 2002, 34t, 34b, 35t, 35b, 38t, 38b, 42. © Photo CNAC/MNAM Dist. RMN/Bertrand Prévost: 33 © DACS 2002. Mary Evans Picture Library: 30c. Peggy Guggenheim Foundation, Venice: Bridgeman 41t © ARS, NY and DACS, London 2002. Hilbick/AKG London: fr cover bc, 29b. Hulton Archive: 32, 36t. Klee family estate deposited at the Paul Klee Foundation, Museum of Fine Arts Berne: fr cover bl, 6t, 6b, 7b, 9b © DACS 2002, 12t, 14b, 36c all © Klee family estate deposited at the Paul Klee Foundation, Museum of Fine Arts Berne. LK Donation, Klee-Museum, Berne: 13 © DACS 2002, 37 © DACS 2002. Paul-Klee-Stiftung, Kunstmuseum Berne: 7c © DACS 2002, 25 © DACS 2002, 39 © DACS 2002. Kunstmuseum, Berne: 18 © L & M Services, Amsterdam 2002. Kunstsammlung, Basel: fr cover c © DACS 2002, 19 © DACS 2002. Musée National d'Art Moderne, Paris: Bridgeman 40. Photograph © 2002 Museum of Modern Art, New York: 27 © DACS 2002. © Renzo Piano Building Workshop/photo Dominique Uldy: 41b. Private Collection: Bridgeman 24t. Private Collection, Switzerland: 15 © DACS 2002. Repro: Rheinisches Bildarchiv, Cologne: 30t detail © DACS 2002, 31 © DACS 2002. Schütze/Rodemann/AKG London: 26c. Sprengel Museum, Hannover: 21 © DACS 2002 Staatsgalerie Moderner Kunst, Munich: Blauel/Gnamm/Artothek 20c. Städtische Galerie im Lenbachhaus, Munich: 11 © DACS 2002, 17 © DACS 2002; AKG London 16t © ADAGP, Paris and DACS, London 2002. Superstock: 14c. Vatican Museums & Galleries, Vatican City: Bridgeman 10c. Victoria & Albert Museum Picture Library, London: 12c.

Whilst every attempt has been made to clear copyright
should there be any inadvertentomission please apply
in the first instance to the publisher regarding rectification.

Contents

Who was Paul Klee?

Paul Klee is one of the most popular artists of the twentieth century. His paintings – full of child-like images of angels, birds, music, inventions, poetry and fabulous creatures – are as exciting today as when they were first created. His talent and unique imagination let us see things in a new way.

'Art does not reproduce the visible but makes visible.'

Paul Klee

◀ Klee (seen here aged 13) did very well at school and particularly liked Greek – he read Greek poetry as a form of relaxation.

▲ Paul in 1899, standing between his mother and father. He also had a sister, Mathilde. Klee's family was loving and supportive throughout his career.

A MAN OF MANY TALENTS

As this book reveals, Paul Klee was not just an artist. He also excelled as a musician, a teacher, a poet and a philosopher. People who knew Klee said that he was a quiet man who played his violin every day, did not talk much and worked all the time at either drawing or writing.

His writing included thousands of pages of diary entries, letters and lecture notes. These help us understand the 9,000 works of art he created during his lifetime.

AN ARTIST OF OPPOSITES

Paul Klee is famous for his use of bright colours, but he painted in many different styles and experimented with lots of techniques throughout his life. For example, earlier in his career he only drew pictures in black, white and shades of grey. He thought that art should break free of history and tradition and find new ways of representing the world. In this quest for innovation, Klee combined all kinds of paints on all kinds of surfaces – he would try anything to make his pictures come alive. Despite the fact that Klee tried so many different ways of painting, his work is always instantly recognisable.

◀ *View from the Elfenau 1896/97. Aus der Elfenau, 1896/97, SB VIII 3,* drawing, 12.2 x 20.2 cm, Paul Klee Stiftung, Kunstmuseum, Berne, Switzerland.
Klee's drawings of nature were very accomplished at an early age – he drew this picture when he was 16.

KLEE THE VIOLINIST

Klee's parents were musicians. His father, Hans, was a music teacher and could play the piano and violin. His mother, Ida, was a trained classical singer. Paul began playing the violin when he was seven years old and was so talented that by the age of 11 he was playing in an orchestra at the Music Society in Berne (his home city). Hans and Ida encouraged Paul to play the violin as they hoped that one day he would be a great musician. But all the time Paul was practising the violin, he was also drawing and writing poetry. When he was a teenager Paul decided that he really wanted to be a painter, but he continued to enjoy music all his life and references to it can be found in many aspects of his art.

▲ Klee, shown here on the far right in 1900, practised the violin every day. This picture was taken in the studio of the private art school Klee attended from 1889-90. The musicians used artists' easels as their music stands.

Becoming a man

Paul Klee was born in 1879. He had German nationality, as his father was German, but grew up in Switzerland. Klee lived in the city of Berne with his parents and his elder sister, Mathilde. When he was four years old, his grandmother gave him a box of chalks and encouraged him to draw.

▲ Berne, Klee's home city. At the turn of the nineteenth and twentieth centuries, it was one of the most cultured and cosmopolitan places in Switzerland.

PRIMARY SCHOOL

When Klee went to school he drew cartoons of his teachers, doodled and made sketchbooks. Some of the pictures he drew as a child are now considered to be important pieces of art. They provide a unique insight into how his drawing developed. Sixty of the pictures Klee drew between the ages of three and 11 survive today – they are worth a great deal of money.

ART SCHOOL

At the age of 19, Klee set off for Munich in Germany. He planned to study at the Munich Art Academy, but was refused entry. Its director thought that Klee did not draw well enough. Disappointed, Klee enrolled at a private art school instead to practise his drawing technique.

Klee did not study very hard. He was leading a kind of double life: on the one side, respectable gentleman, on the other, wild student.

TIMELINE ▶					
18 December 1879	1886	1898	1899	1900	1901
Paul born, the second child of Hans and Ida Klee.	Paul starts primary school.	Paul leaves school and travels to Munich. Studies at a private art school.	Paul meets his future wife, pianist Lily Stumpf.	Klee gains a place at the Munich Academy of Art.	Klee leaves the Academy. He becomes secretly engaged to Lily Stumpf.

'There were even times I didn't turn up at class... In short, I first had to become a man: art would then follow as a matter of course.'

Paul Klee

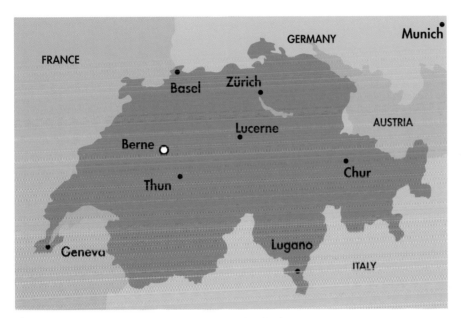

▲ Switzerland is at the heart of Europe. Klee had easy access to Europe's artistic core – France, Germany and Italy. Klee lived in Berne, Switzerland's second city after Zürich.

A DOUBLE LIFE

On the one side, Klee went to concerts, operas and the theatre, played the violin with other musicians and mixed with sensible, intellectual people – many of them friends of his parents. But with his art school friends, Klee spent all his money, stayed out all night, got drunk and had lots of girlfriends!

In October 1900, Klee finally gained entrance to the Munich Academy. However, he did not change his reckless way of life; he attended very few classes and did not enjoy them. Klee left the Academy in March 1901, only months after he joined.

PAUL AND LILY

In 1899, while at a musical evening given by friends of his parents, Klee met Lily Stumpf (1876-1946), a pianist. They began going to concerts and playing music together. Soon after he met Lily, Klee wrote in his diary that he wanted to marry her. But Lily came from a respectable middle-class family and her father, a doctor, was not pleased that she was going out with an artist. After leaving the Munich Academy in 1901, Klee and Lily became secretly engaged, but did not marry for another five years, partly because Lily's parents were against it and partly because Klee wanted to establish himself as an artist.

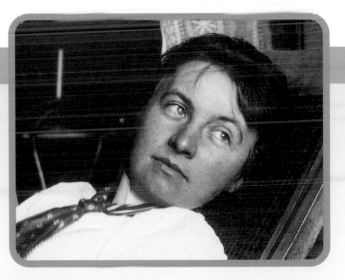

▲ This photograph of Lily Stumpf was taken by Klee in 1906, the year in which they were finally married.

Fabulous inventions

▲ Orville and Wilbur Wright in their plane the Wright Flyer. The Wright Brothers completed the first power-driven flight on 17th December 1903 at Kitty Hawk, North Carolina, USA. They were in the air for 12 seconds and travelled 36 metres.

FLYING FANATICS

Winged Hero is one of the first pictures Paul sold. It is the third picture in his *Inventions* series and was inspired by the efforts of the Wright brothers to build and fly the first aeroplane. Klee's creature is a hero because it tries to fly when all the odds are against it – it is rooted to the earth by one leg, it has only one wing and its arm is broken. Despite this, Klee wrote in his diary, the creature remains 'loyal to the idea of flying'. Klee had a life-long interest in flight and birds appear in hundreds of his pictures (see pages 21 and 27).

In October 1901, Klee travelled to Italy with a school friend to see the work of the Old Masters – great Italian artists such as Leonardo da Vinci (1452-1519), Michelangelo Buonarroti (1475-1564) and Raphael (1483-1520). Despite mixed reactions to what he saw, he found it an inspiring trip.

When he returned in 1902, he went to live in Berne with his parents. Klee earned money by giving drawing lessons and playing in an orchestra. When he had saved enough money, he travelled to Munich to visit Lily.

◄ During his trip to Italy, Klee visited the Sistine Chapel in the Vatican City in Rome. It is famous for its ceiling (left), elaborately painted by Michelangelo Buonarroti between 1509 and 1512. The ceiling had been admired for generations, but Klee hated it – he felt that this was exactly the kind of art he wanted to move away from in his quest to create something new, exciting and modern.

THE *INVENTIONS*

In July 1903, Klee began work on a series of etchings that he called the *Inventions*. He created strange, fantastical creatures and gave them names such as *Winged Hero* (right). Klee worked on the *Inventions* for two years and etched ten creatures in all. He felt that the *Inventions* were his best work so far as an adult artist.

TIMELINE ▶

October 1901	May 1902	July 1903	1903	1905
Klee travels to Italy. He visits Milan, Pisa, Rome, Naples and Florence.	Klee returns to Berne, Switzerland.	Klee starts working on the *Inventions*.	The Wright brothers (USA) make the first powered flight in the *Wright Flyer*.	Klee finishes the *Inventions*.

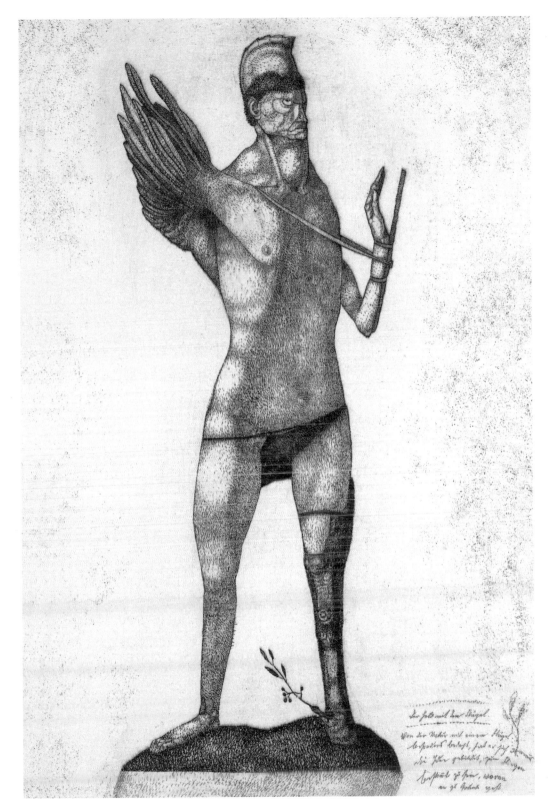

Winged Hero, 1905
Der Held mit dem Flügel, 1905, 38

etching 25.4 x 15.7 cm City Gallery, Lenbachhaus, Munich, Germany

Klee's *Inventions* are etchings. Etchings are pictures drawn into a wax-covered metal sheet, called a plate. The plate is then covered in acid, which eats into the metal where the wax has been scratched away. The wax is removed and the plate covered with ink and pressed onto paper to make the picture.

Drawing on glass

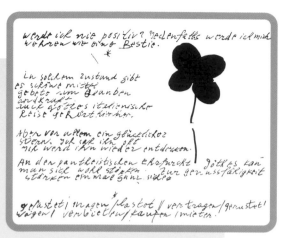

▲ An extract from Klee's diaries. They were written in German.

In July 1905, Klee began drawing on glass instead of paper. We know from his diary entries that to create pictures such as *My Father*, he covered a pane of glass with a thin layer of black paint. When it had dried, he used a needle to scratch into the paint right through to the surface of the glass. When he was happy with his drawing, Klee covered the back of the glass with white paint, filling in all the scratches.

KLEE'S DIARIES

Klee kept diaries between 1898 and 1918. In them he wrote about everything from poetry, politics, and his family to other artists, music, his theories about painting and his struggles to master art techniques. Reading Klee's diaries are the closest we will ever get to hearing his voice and we learn a great deal about his personal thoughts and ideas.

> *'I am not here to reflect the surface... I reflect the innermost heart.'*
>
> Paul Klee's diary

Traditional Bavarian ▶ glass painting, an example of which is shown here, is called *Hinterglasmalerei* – meaning 'reverse' or 'behind' glass painting. This kind of painting was popular in Bavaria from around 1680 until about 1880.

DOING THINGS DIFFERENTLY

Drawing on glass is a very old art in Bavaria, the part of Germany Klee lived in when he went to art school. But traditional Bavarian glass painting involves initially covering the glass with white paint and then painting black over the engraved image. Klee reversed this process. Bavarian glass also often featured colour which Klee was not interested in at all. Klee wanted to show that history was important by using a long-practised technique. But by upsetting its traditions, he also showed he was not going to follow the established rules and he was determined to find his own way of constructing shape, form, space, pattern and texture.

TIMELINE ▶

1905	1905	1906	June 1906
Klee travels to Paris with an artist friend, Louis Moilliet (1880-1962), to visit the Louvre museum. Also sees the work of some of the Impressionists.	Klee begins drawing his glass-pane pictures. He will produce 57 between now and 1912.	Klee goes to Berlin, visits the National Gallery. He is not impressed by the old-fashioned art he sees there.	Klee's *Inventions* are exhibited at the Munich Secession.

My Father, 1906
Mein Vater, 1906, 23

glass-pane 31.8 x 29.3 cm Schenkung LK, Klee-Museum, Berne, Switzerland
Klee made 57 glass-pane drawings between 1905 and 1912, including one of his
father in 1906. Klee really enjoyed his new way of working because it combined
drawing and etching, the two things he was already good at. He described the
technique as 'ingenious' in his diary.

Black watercolours

In 1906, Klee finally married Lily and in 1907 they had their first and only child, Felix. At the time, Klee was applying himself to watercolour painting but, unlike most artists, he used only dark shades and colours. In his black watercolours, Klee experimented with tone – shades of light and dark – just as he had in his glass-pane pictures.

AN UNUSUAL MARRIAGE

Paul and Lily married on 15 September 1906. The newly-weds moved into a three-roomed flat in Munich. Klee found it difficult to earn money so, when Felix was born in 1907, he became a househusband – something that was completely unheard of at the time. He turned the kitchen into a studio where he could paint and look after Felix at the same time. Klee bought all the shopping, cleaned the house and cooked the family meals. Meanwhile, Lily supported the family by giving up to 50 piano lessons a week.

◀ Many people play the game of seeing pictures in cloud formations. Klee wanted people to play the same game with his art.

CHILD'S PLAY
The black watercolours were a step for Klee towards a way of painting that started as a childhood game. Aged nine, he had stared at the shapes and patterns on the marble-topped tables in his uncle's restaurant. His mind had made pictures from these random shapes, in the same way people make pictures by looking at groups of clouds in the sky. Klee wanted his art to have the same effect as his childhood game.

'The market was open, and the butchers had a laugh as we walked by their stands.'

Paul Klee on his wedding day

▲ Paul and Lily in Berne in 1906, the year of their marriage.

TIMELINE ▶

15 September 1906	30 November 1907	1908	1909
Lily and Paul get married.	Lily and Paul's only child, Felix, is born.	Klee sees paintings by the Post-Impressionist Vincent van Gogh (1853-90) on show in Munich.	Klee sees pictures by the Post-Impressionists Paul Cézanne (1839-1906) and Henri Matisse (1869-1954).

Child in a Highchair (Small Boy), 1908
Kind im Klappstuhl (Kleiner), 1908, 57

drawing in black watercolour 15.3 x 15.3 cm Private Collection, Switzerland

Klee's etchings and glass-pane drawings took a long time to complete but watercolour paint dries very quickly so the black watercolours were 'instant' pictures for the artist. His use of dark colours meant they often looked like drawings rather than paintings. Klee found looking after Felix, who is shown above, kept him away from his art – but his son obviously proved useful as a model!

The Blue Riders

▲ *Impression III*, Wassily Kandinsky, 1911. The finger-like shapes are people at a concert but the picture is mainly an 'impression' of a huge yellow sound – the music – filling the hall.

ABSTRACT PICTURES

The Blue Riders painted abstract pictures – pictures that are not recognisable as anything in the world around us (turn to page 31 to see one of Klee's most abstract pictures). Amongst other things, they took inspiration from children's drawings and Oriental, folk and tribal art rather than the Old Masters (see page 10). They also believed that abstract pictures could reveal a spiritual aspect of the world, an idea expressed by Kandinsky in his book, *Concerning the Spiritual in Art* (1912).

In 1910 Klee had an exhibition of 56 of his pictures, which was shown in three Swiss galleries. At two of the galleries he sold only a handful of pictures. At the third gallery people hated his work and the exhibition closed within a few days.

A NEW SOCIETY OF ARTISTS

The public may not have liked Klee's work, but other artists did. Thanks to his exhibitions, Klee met the German artists August Macke (1887-1914) and Franz Marc (1880-1916) and the Russian artist Wassily Kandinsky (1866-1944). These men were part of a group of Munich-based artists called the *Der Blaue Reiter* (German for 'The Blue Riders').

'Kandinsky wants to organise a new society of artists.'
Paul Klee

◀ Founder of the Blue Riders, Wassily Kandinsky, at his desk.

The Blue Riders were founded in Munich by Wassily Kandinsky in 1911 and were active until 1916. Klee was invited to join them by Kandinsky later in 1911, an event which forced him to take more notice of Munich's more avant-garde artists.

TIMELINE ▶

1910	1911	Autumn 1911	1912	2-18 April 1912	1913
Klee's first one-man show.	Klee keeps a catalogue of his work. He numbers each one after the date it was made.	Kandinsky founds The Blue Riders in Munich. Klee is invited to join the group.	Second Blue Rider Exhibition, Klee shows 17 pictures. The Blue Rider almanac is published.	Lily and Paul go to Paris where they meet the artist Robert Delaunay (see page 18).	Klee shows his work at the *Galerie der Sturm* (The Storm Gallery) in Berlin.

Flower Stand, Watering Can and Bucket, 1910
Blumensteg, Gießkanne u Eimer, 1910, 47

watercolour on paper 13.9 x 13.3 cm City Gallery, Lenbachhaus, Munich, Germany

This watercolour appeared in Klee's 1910 exhibition. The subject matter of the picture is very ordinary – it features everyday objects in an unremarkable setting – and whilst the objects in the title are easy to recognise, it is obvious that Klee has tried to simplify their forms and outlines into more solid blocks of colour. This approach to art coincided with some of the ideas of the Blue Riders, so it is easy to see why his work attracted their attention.

An inspirational holiday

In April 1914, Klee travelled with his artist friends Louis Moilliet and August Macke to Tunisia in North Africa for a 17-day painting holiday. This holiday was to change Klee's art forever.

PAINTING IN COLOUR

Klee was inspired by everything he saw in Tunisia – the landscape, the architecture and the sunlight. For the first time, Klee enjoyed painting with colour, putting into practice ideas he had discussed with French artist, Robert Delaunay, in 1912 (see panel). He mixed bright watercolours and placed them next to each other in shimmering, transparent blocks. Then he added a few dark lines of paint to represent trees, animals or people. Klee was excited. He felt he was a painter at last.

▲ *Formes Circulaires*, Robert and Sonia Delaunay, 1912. The husband and wife team created their own type of Cubism that used colour and shapes to represent nature.

'Colour possesses me. I don't have to pursue it. It will possess me always, I know it. That is the meaning of this happy hour: Colour and I are one. I am a painter. '

Paul Klee writing in Tunisia

ROBERT DELAUNAY (1885-1941)

Klee and Macke met Robert Delaunay in Paris in 1912 and discussed his ideas about colour. Delaunay worked with his wife Sonia. They created light in their art by putting contrasting colours next to each other, not by varying the tone of one particular colour or combination of colours. They called this style of painting Orphism.

TIMELINE ▶

5-22 April 1914	28 June 1914	July 1914	August 1914
Klee goes to Tunisia with August Macke and Louis Moilliet. Klee paints in full colour for the first time.	Archduke Ferdinand of Austria is assassinated in Sarajevo, Serbia.	Austria declares war on Serbia, with German support. Russia and France align with Serbia.	World War I begins (see pages 22-3). Macke and Marc join the German army.

Motiv aus Hammamet 1914 48

Motif from Hammamet, 1914
Motiv aus Hammamet, 1914, 48

watercolour and pencil on paper 20.3 x 15.7 cm Oeffentliche Kunstsammlung, Basle, Switzerland
Compare this painting with the black watercolour on page 15. In the portrait of Felix, Klee creates
a picture using tone and includes the detail so it is easy to tell what the picture is. Whereas here,
Klee creates a picture using pure colour. He only suggests the shape of the houses, the colour of the
sky and the size of the fields – he lets your imagination fill in the rest.

Painting through a war

▲ An aeroplane at a German air-base in World War I. Aeroplanes were new in warfare and mainly used for reconnaissance – to track enemy movements. However, some aircraft could also be used to bomb enemy targets on the ground.

ON AN AIR-BASE

By the time Klee was conscripted, many Munich artists had already died. The authorities arranged for other Munich artists to be kept away from the fighting, so Klee was sent to an air-base to work as a clerk. He painted in his desk drawer when no one was looking and worked when he was off-duty in a room near the base that he rented as a studio. When painting, he could forget his surroundings and the war. Once, he wrote in his diary, he was so engrossed in his work that he was amazed when he looked down at 'his cruel war-like boots'.

Three months after Klee returned from Tunisia war broke out in Europe. August Macke and Franz Marc immediately joined the German army and went to fight. Tragically Macke was killed only four weeks later.

Still inspired by his trip to Tunisia, Klee stayed in Munich and worked every day, producing 475 pictures between 1914 and 1915. Klee made a few drawings and etchings related to the subject of fighting or politics, but – unlike his friend Franz Marc – he tried to ignore the war as much as possible.

▲ *Fighting Forms*, Franz Marc, 1914. Marc reflects the furious activity created by battle with swirling paint and red and black areas crashing together in the centre.

DEVASTATION AND SUCCESS

In 1916, Marc was killed at Verdun when a splinter from an artillery shell hit him in the head. Klee was devastated. Then, only seven days later, he was conscripted by the German government – he had no choice but to join the army (see panel). However, he carried on painting and showed his work, with its new colourful style, in an exhibition in 1917. The public loved it – at the age of 38, Klee was finally a success.

TIMELINE ▶

September 1914	4 March 1916	11 March 1916	February 1917	11 November 1918
August Macke is killed fighting on the front line.	Franz Marc killed in the trenches at Verdun in France (see pages 22-3).	Klee is conscripted. After military training camp, he works as a clerk.	Klee has a one-man exhibition at *Galerie der Sturm* in Berlin.	Germany is defeated. World War I is over.

Flower Myth, 1918
Blumenmythos, 1918, 82

watercolour on shirt cloth with chalk ground, mounted on newspaper, mounted on
cardboard, with silver-bronze frame 29 x 15.8 cm Sprengel Museum, Hanover, Germany
While working at the air force base Klee watched planes taking off and landing all day.
Sometimes he saw them crash. In *Flower Myth* a bird plummets towards the earth, its eyes
huge with fear, its wings as weak and stiff as the wings of a paper aeroplane.

World War I (1914-18)

While Klee was attending art school at the turn of the century, Europe's major powers became involved in a race to see which country could expand its army and navy to be the biggest and the best. This arms race led to a very hostile atmosphere in Europe and, by 1914, two armed-camps had emerged: the Central Powers – Germany and Austria-Hungary – and the Allies – France, Russia, Belgium and Britain. It took only an isolated incident for a full-scale war to break out.

▲ The Battle of Verdun took place between February and June 1916. The French repelled a German attack, but over half a million soldiers were killed in all. One of them was Klee's friend Franz Marc.

◀ This map shows the countries of Europe during 1914, with the main European Allied Powers marked in red and those of the Central Powers in yellow.

THE SPARK

On 28 June 1914, a Serb nationalist shot Archduke Francis Ferdinand of Austria-Hungary in Sarajevo, Serbia. The Archduke was the heir to the thrones of both Austria and Hungary. Encouraged by Germany, Austria declared war on Serbia, then Russia offered Serbia its support. The tensions in Europe bubbled over. Germany declared war on Russia and France and invaded Belgium. Britain declared war on Germany because of its invasion of Belgium. In little over a month, most of Europe was at war.

TIMELINE ▶

28 June 1914	28 July 1914	August 1914	1915	1916	1917	11 November 1918
Archduke Francis Ferdinand shot at Sarajevo.	Austria-Hungary declares war on Serbia.	Germany declares war on Russia and France and invades Belgium. Britain declares war on Germany.	Italy joins the war on the side of the Allies.	Battles of Verdun and the Somme.	The USA joins the war on the side of Britain. Russian Revolution.	The Armistice is signed. The war is over, Germany is defeated.

A WAR TO END ALL WARS?

Most of the European powers who entered the war believed it would be short, but their armies were very evenly balanced. The new 'trench warfare' (see panel) led to long, drawn out battles over small stretches of land. What would become known as the Great War and then World War I lasted for more than four years. It stretched across all of Europe, into Asia and Africa and involved 65 million soldiers. By Armistice Day on 11 November 1918, 8.5 million men had died fighting and 20 million were wounded. For those who were left behind, like Klee, there was a high price to pay for the devastation. As losers, Germany in particular had to meet the vast cost of the war and its new Weimar Republic faced a very difficult future.

▲ Wounded British and German soldiers march together down a street in St Quentin, France, 1918. No one had expected a long war.

NEW WAYS OF FIGHTING

World War I saw the introduction of new fighting machines, including submarines, tanks and aeroplanes. World War I also saw the introduction of new methods of warfare, such as chemical warfare, in the form of poison gas, and trench warfare.

The trenches were long ditches in the ground that opposing armies lived in, defended and tried to take from each other. The land in between the lines of trenches was called no-man's land. Conditions in the trenches were often horrific, filthy, with plagues of rats and lice, and wet. In an attack, men went 'over the top' into no-man's land, barbed wire and enemy gunfire.

Trench warfare gave rise to the longest battles in history, involving greater numbers of men and casualties than had ever been engaged in fighting before. The most famous trench battles were in France on the Somme and at Ypres and Verdun.

PENDANT LA BATAILLE DE LA MEUSE
Une charge à la baïonnette

▲ Fighting in the trenches was fierce and bloody. This cover from the French magazine *Le Petit Journal* illustrates an attack by French troops on a German line.

Poems in paint

◀ *Blossoms*, Hongshou Chen (1768-1821). In the Chinese language words are written in characters. These do not work like an alphabet: rather than being individual letters, characters represent whole words, or even concepts.

In 1916, while Klee was away on military service, Lily sent him a book of Chinese poetry. Klee adored Lily's gift and it inspired him to find a way of placing words in paintings over the coming years. Klee left the army in 1919 and returned to Munich.

POETRY AND PAINTING

In written Chinese, the meaning of a poem depends partly on where the words are positioned on the page. Klee took this idea and applied it to colour instead of words. In *Once Emerged from the Grey of Night...*, Klee linked important letters with colours by putting them in the same squares or patches of colour over and over again. The letters then turn into words, the words become lines of poetry and the lines become a verse. The letters sitting in their blocks of colour became the structure and subject of the painting rather than the poem itself.

KLEE THE POET

It is thought that Klee wrote the poem in the painting *Once Emerged from the Grey of Night...* The poem is written in German. This is an English translation:

Once emerged from the grey
of night
Then heavy and dear
And strong from the fire
In the evening full of God and
bent.
Now ethereally surrounded by
shuddering blue
Floating away over firm
To clever stars.

TIMELINE ▶

December 1918	February 1919	1919
Klee goes home to Munich and spends Christmas with Lily and Felix.	Klee is allowed to leave the army.	German architect Walter Gropius (1883-1969) sets up the Bauhaus art school in the German city of Weimar.

Once Emerged from the Grey of Night . . ., 1918
Einst dem Grau der Nacht enttaucht . . ., 1918, 17

watercolour and pen and ink on paper 22.6 x 15.8 cm Paul Klee Stiftung, Kunstmuseum, Berne, Switzerland
All the 'As' in *Once Emerged from the Grey of Night. . .* have the colour yellow as their background. The middle of the picture has 'hot' squares of yellow and red that signify the fire mentioned in the poem.

Klee the teacher

▲ Klee in his studio in 1920. He painted many pictures at the same time, usually working on a different image each day.

MECHANICAL BIRDS

Klee loved nature all his life and thought that it was important for people to learn from the natural world. In *The Twittering Machine*, Klee pokes fun at people who ignore the wonders of nature and believe that machines can do everything. The imaginary machine in the picture is made up of four mechanical birds sitting on a thin bar which is attached to a crankshaft. If you turn the shaft the birds will sing – but, as Klee believed, everyone knows that no machine can make a sound as beautiful as real birds singing.

At home again with Lily and Felix after the war, Klee was happy at the prospect of being a full-time artist again. However, in 1920 Walter Gropius, a German architect who had set up an art school called the Bauhaus (see pages 28-9), wrote to Klee and offered him a job as a teacher in his new school in Weimar (it later moved to Dessau). Klee eagerly accepted. For the first time, he had a steady job that gave him a regular income and the free use of a studio.

LECTURE NOTES

Some of Klee's most important work at the Bauhaus took the form of the lectures in basic design he gave to all students in their Foundation year (see page 28). These lectures contain Klee's theories of art. Between 1925 and 1931, Klee filled over 3,000 pages of drawings and text with his lecture notes. He also wrote essays and, of course, continued painting.

▲ Klee's home at the Bauhaus school in Dessau which he shared with Kandinsky (who also taught at the school). It was designed by Gropius.

'The artist is a man, himself nature and a part of nature...'

Paul Klee, from his essay On Modern Art, 1924

TIMELINE ▶

29 October 1920	1920	10 January 1921	September 1921	1921	1922
Klee is offered a teaching post at the Bauhaus in Weimar, Germany.	Klee is now famous. His art dealer, Hans Goltz, organises an exhibition of 326 of his pictures.	Klee begins teaching at the Bauhaus.	Felix Klee, aged 13, becomes the youngest student at the Bauhaus.	Klee's mother, Ida, dies.	Wassily Kandinsky (see page 16) becomes a teacher at the Bauhaus.

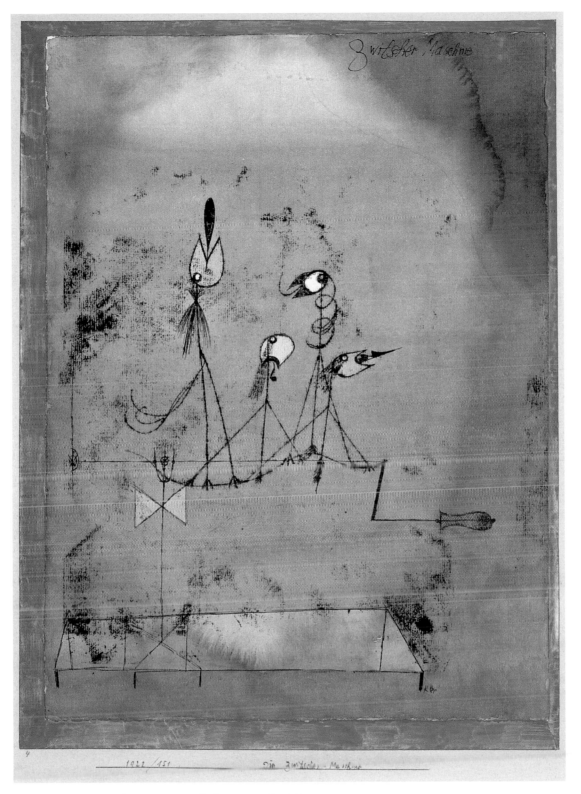

The Twittering Machine, 1922
Die Zwitscher-Maschine, 1922, 151

watercolour and oil transfer drawing on paper, mounted on cardboard 41.3 x 30.5 cm
Museum of Modern Art, New York, Mrs John D. Rockefeller Jr Purchase Fund

The Twittering Machine is an example of Klee's oil-transfer technique, a way of combining drawing and painting, which he developed at the Bauhaus. Klee transferred an image he had drawn in pencil onto a painted canvas by tracing the pencil line over a page coated with black oil, pressing the oil onto the canvas.

The Bauhaus

When Klee arrived to teach at the Bauhaus in Weimar in January 1921, the school was already famous. After World War I, many German artists felt that art and design could help to make the world a better place for ordinary people, in particular by using mass-production techniques now available in industry. The Bauhaus was the art school where these ideals were to become reality.

◀ The Professors of Painting and Graphic Art at the Bauhaus, 1928. Klee is on the far right, Kandinsky second from left. Most of the Bauhaus's lecturers were famous artists in their own right.

A STRONG FOUNDATION

In their first year at the school, students tried several disciplines including metalwork, typography, pottery, sculpture and weaving. This helped them develop a number of skills. They then chose the discipline in which they were most interested. Gropius called this year a Foundation year – an important Bauhaus innovation. Up until this time, art students studied only drawing and painting. However, art schools all over the world soon adopted Gropius' idea and today all art students have to complete a Foundation year.

GOOD DESIGN

The Bauhaus wanted good design to be available to everyone at affordable prices. Gropius believed that machine-produced objects had aesthetic qualities equal to those that were hand-made. At the time this was an unusual idea.

▲ Walter Gropius (1883-1969) fought in World War I. An influential architect, he set up the Bauhaus school in 1920 and was its director until 1928. In 1934, Gropius emigrated to England and then to the USA in 1937.

THE BAUHAUS STYLE

Bauhaus designs are very distinctive – they are very functional, have little decoration and tend to be made of modern materials such as steel and glass. Bauhaus objects look modern today even though they were designed over 75 years ago. Bauhaus designs are all around us in schools, offices and homes.

'Art itself cannot be taught, but craftsmanship can.'

Walter Gropius

THE BAUHAUS IS CLOSED

The Bauhaus was unpopular with the Weimar town council who did not approve of its unusual teaching methods; residents were also fed up with the rowdy behaviour of the students! Weimar stopped giving money to the school in 1925 and it moved to Dessau. After seven years the Dessau town council closed the school and it moved to Berlin. After a year in Berlin the Nazis (see pages 34-5) shut the Bauhaus down – it was different and was therefore viewed as a threat. By the time it closed its doors the Bauhaus had become the most influential art school of the twentieth century.

◀ This Bauhaus chair was designed in 1929-30, but it is a style that has been adapted and copied ever since.

GROPIUS THE ARCHITECT

When the Bauhaus moved to Dessau, Walter Gropius designed a new building (pictured right) for the school as well as Masters' houses for all the teachers, including one for Paul Klee and Wassily Kandinsky (see page 26). These new buildings illustrate the style of the Bauhaus. The new college contained a complicated series of workshops, studios, showrooms, offices, accommodation and a library and yet the exterior of the building is very simple – it was just a block of steel, glass and concrete. This building influenced factory, school and housing architecture all over Europe and America for years to come.

▲ 'Bauhaus' means 'House of Building' in German. Walter Gropius believed that art and crafts should be taught in the same place (in one 'house') and that they should have a practical use (to 'build') in day-to-day life.

Egyptian landscape

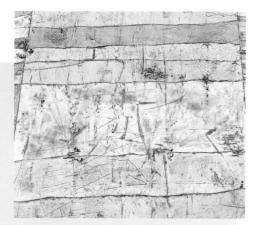

▲ This detail from *Highway and Byways* shows the rough texture of its surface. Klee always carefully chose the materials he painted on to suit his subject matter.

MATERIALS

Highway and Byways not only looks as rough as the earth of a newly-ploughed field but also feels it. Klee covered the canvas in rough plaster to achieve this effect. In an effort to make the surfaces of his paintings appropriate to their subjects, Klee painted on different materials including: transparent wax paper, glass, metal, newspaper, cardboard, shirt cloth, canvas, writing paper, plaster and watercolour paper. He also made his own paintbrushes and decorated his paintboxes with shells and stones.

Klee felt that he was only useful as a teacher if he was still an active artist, so he painted throughout his time at the Bauhaus. In between teaching and painting, Klee went on holiday to places such as Brittany and Corsica. Then in 1928, to celebrate his 50th birthday, Klee travelled to North Africa once more. This time he went to Egypt.

'During this Egyptian trip, Klee worked very little, perhaps not at all. He merely stored up impressions.'

Felix Klee

▲ Klee visited the pyramids and temples of ancient Egypt.

A NET OF PAINT

Klee's time in Egypt inspired *Highway and Byways*, one of his most famous paintings. In it, he suggests ploughed fields by placing horizontal blocks of colour next to each other – like the stone blocks used to build the pyramids. A straight highroad runs through the middle of the picture, at the top the blue of the sky. Fields and roads are solid things but Klee makes them look like a delicate, floating net of paint.

TIMELINE ▶

1923	1923	January 1924	26 December 1924	1925	December 1928
Klee's work is shown in the Bauhaus exhibition.	The first 'magic square' pictures are completed (see pages 32-3).	Klee's first exhibition in America opens in New York.	The Bauhaus is closed in Weimar.	The Bauhaus reopens in Dessau. Klee's first exhibition in Paris.	Klee travels to Egypt for a month.

Highway and Byways, 1929
Hauptweg und Nebenwege, 1929, 90

oil with a plaster ground on canvas 83.7 x 67.5 cm Museum Ludwig, Cologne, Germany
The fields in *Highway and Byways* also look like collections of roads. The balance between
thick and thin 'roads' gives an impression of movement.

Magic musical squares

Klee's time at the Bauhaus was his most productive in terms of art. Amongst his large output was a series of pictures that attempted to describe the sound of music. These pictures are known as the 'magic square' paintings.

SEEING MUSIC

The black, grey and white rectangles in *Rhythmical* represent a three-beat bar of music. When you look at the picture your eyes combine all the 'notes' represented by each square of colour and you can 'see', or even 'hear', a continuous rhythm.

What do you think of when you look at *Rhythmical*? Many people say this picture reminds them of a jazz band or of a loud brass instrument, such as a trombone, repeating the same three notes over and over again.

▲ Jazz was very popular when Klee painted *Rhythmical* but it was still considered avant-garde music.

'One day [at the Bauhaus] I heard a strange rhythmical stamping of feet. When I met Klee in the hallway I asked him: "Did you hear that odd noise just now?" He laughed and said: "Ah – did you notice? I was painting and suddenly, I don't know why – I had to dance."'

Georg Muche, artist and Bauhaus teacher

MUSIC AND SQUARES

The rows of coloured squares in Klee's magic square pictures represent the ascending or descending notes of chords. Klee thought that each square was like a member of a choir with its own note to sing and that, when all the squares were combined, the picture would 'sing' with one voice.

When you look at a magic square painting, your eyes can *see* the whole sound (the whole image) as well as individual notes (the separate squares) – just as when you listen to music you can *hear* the whole sound as well as individual notes. You could almost dance to this painting!

TIMELINE ▶

1929	October 1929	1930	1 April 1931
Exhibitions of Klee's work are held in Berlin and Paris in honour of his 50th birthday.	The New York stock market crashes. The Great Depression begins.	The Berlin exhibition of Klee's work travels to the Museum of Modern Art in New York.	Klee resigns from the Bauhaus.

Rhythmical, 1930
Rhyth-misches, 1930, 203

oil on canvas with original frame 69 x 50 cm Georges Pompidou Centre,
Musée National d'Art Moderne, Paris, France

**Look at the squares in *Rhythmical*. The areas of grey force some of the black and white squares,
or 'notes', to blur into each other. These squares represent slurred notes in the music's rhythm.**

The rise of the Nazis

A unemployment queue in Germany, 1930. After World War I the victorious Allies imposed fines on the German state to punish it. These fines contributed to Germany's high unemployment and galloping inflation.

While Klee was working at the Bauhaus, the political and economic situation in Germany was changing dramatically. Burdened with debts from World War I, the Weimar Republic struggled to rebuild the German economy. The New York stock exchange crash of 1929 made the situation far worse, taking the Western world into the Great Depression. In Germany, 60 per cent of the workforce were unemployed. Inflation was out of control and people were starving. The Germans began to look to a more radical solution to their problems – the Nazis.

THE NATIONAL SOCIALISTS

The Nazis were members of the National Socialist German Workers' Party led by Adolf Hitler. The Nazis believed that only the power and wealth of Germany was important. Individuals had to dedicate their lives to their country. However, the Nazis were also extremely racist, believing that only Germans of Ayran descent were 'true' Germans. In particular, they blamed the Jews of Germany for its economic crisis.

In the German elections of 1930, 6.5 million people voted for the Nazis. By 1932, it was 14 million – making them the largest party in the German Parliament. In 1933, Hitler became head of a coalition government and the Nazis took control of Germany.

A poster advertising a Nazi party rally at Nuremberg in 1933. The figure of Hitler dominates the picture.

TIMELINE ▶

September 1930	30 January 1933	23 March 1933	1 April 1933	10 May 1933	23 June 1933	29 August 1933
The Nazis take 107 seats in German national elections.	The Nazis come to power, with Hitler at the head of a coalition government.	Hitler is given full powers to govern Germany by the 'Enabling Bill'.	Hitler orders that Jewish businesses be boycotted.	The Nazis burn books that they consider to be unpatriotic.	Hitler bans all opposition parties.	First Jews sent to concentration camps.

One of the first laws introduced by the Nazis was one forcing Jews to wear yellow stars. By 1945, six million Jewish men, women and children would be dead, murdered by the Nazis. This event is called the Holocaust.

NAZI POLICIES

At first the policies of the Nazi government worked. Unemployment was reduced and the economy stabilised. But this security came at a price. Hitler sought to rid his country of people who did not represent the 'purity' of the German (Ayran) race. This included disabled people, mental patients, and 'non-Germans' – Jews, gypsies and Slavs. People who couldn't prove their Aryan ancestory were hounded out of their jobs, denied their rights, or, in the case of Jews in particular, taken to concentration camps to face starvation, overwork and death.

The Nazis ruthlessly supressed political opposition but their desire to control extended to all areas of life, including the arts. Musicians, actors, film-makers and artists had to swear allegiance to Nazi principles. Klee, never overtly 'political', was no exception.

▲ Adolf Hitler greets the crowds at Nuremberg, 1933. The Nazi leader was a vegetarian, an animal lover and an artist – but he was also one of the biggest murderers of the twentieth century.

ADOLF HITLER (1889-1945)

Adolf Hitler was born in Austria. He joined the German army, having left school at 16, and won several medals for bravery. But Hitler was disillusioned by Germany's defeat in World War I and joined the Nazis – becoming leader of the party in 1925. After an unsuccessful attempt to overthrow the German government, Hitler was sent to prison for a year where he wrote *Mein Kampf* (My Struggle), an outline of his political theories that included his deep hatred of Jews.

Hitler was a charismatic leader and his emotional speeches and patriotic belief in the 'Fatherland' captivated many Germans, bringing him and the Nazis to power in 1933. However, his agressive foreign policy led to World War II, while Germany's defeat in 1945 led to Hitler's suicide. It was only then that the world finally realised the true extent of his racist policies and the horror of the Holocaust.

Artists under attack

▲ A community of artists and journalists in Berlin being arrested by the Nazis, March 1933. Their work was confiscated.

In 1931 Klee left the Bauhaus and took up a new teaching job as Professor of Art at the Art Academy in Dusseldorf. He gave fewer lectures so he had more time to paint, but this all changed when the Nazis came to power in 1933. They replaced the Director of the Art Academy with one of their supporters and began to ban the sale of modern art (affecting Klee's income). Hitler also demanded that all teachers prove their Aryan birth. As Klee tried to find the necessary documents, he was asked to prove he was loyal to the Nazi party. Klee refused to do this and was sacked.

THE NAZIS CLOSE IN

The Nazis swiftly took control of the media, the cinema and theatres. They bullied artists and writers who criticised them and made it hard for them to make a living. In 1933, while Klee was in Dusseldorf, the Nazis broke into a flat he still kept in Dessau. When Klee returned, he found his apartment turned upside down. The Nazis took away three baskets of his letters, his lecture notes and other documents. This deeply upset Klee. Later, he asked a friend to pack up what was left in the flat because he could not face returning to it and its reminders of the Nazi raid.

◄ Paul and Lily in Berne, 1935, with their cat Bimbo. The Klees were relieved to be safe from the Nazis in Switzerland, but Klee was sad to leave behind his teaching and the conversation of artist friends.

RETURNING TO SWITZERLAND

Life had become extremely difficult for artists in Germany and many left the country. Klee was reluctant to go, but Lily saw the danger he was in and persuaded him that the family should return to Switzerland. 'I don't want bitterness to creep in,' Klee wrote to Felix as he packed to leave, but as *Struck from the List* reveals, he was clearly very upset.

TIMELINE ▶

1931	1932	March 1933	April 1933	December 1933
Klee takes up a new teaching job at the Art Academy in Dusseldorf.	The Bauhaus is closed in Dessau and moves to Berlin.	Klee's Dessau house is searched by the Nazi authorities. His art is denounced in the press.	Klee is sacked from his job at the Academy. The Nazis close down the Bauhaus.	The Klees move back to Paul's father's house in Berne, Switzerland.

Struck from the List, 1933
Von der Liste gestrichen, 1933, 424

oils on transparent wax paper 31.5 x 24 cm Schenkung LK, Klee-Museum, Berne, Switzerland

This self-portrait is a powerful indication of Klee's state of mind on leaving Germany. The big X across the back of Klee's head suggests isolation and exclusion. His eyes are closed in frustration and there appears to be a pool of tears beneath his left eye.

Exile in Switzerland

▲ Goebbels, the Nazi Minister for Propaganda, inspects the Degenerate Art Show in 1937.

'DEGENERATE' ART

The Nazis did not let up in their campaign against modern artists. In 1937, Goebbels, the Nazi Minister for Propaganda, ordered the organisation of an exhibition of all the art they hated. They called it the Degenerate Art Show. It included 17 of Klee's pictures, which were described in the exhibition catalogue as 'the work of a sick mind'.

The Nazis confiscated thousands of paintings, including Klee's. Goering, a senior Nazi party official and Commander of the Luftwaffe, the German airforce, either sold them to art galleries abroad or publicly burned them as a warning to other artists. Klee's paintings were returned to his family after the war.

In Switzerland, Paul soon became depressed. Not only did he feel exiled from his friends and work, but he started to worry about not having enough money. Then, at the end of 1935, Klee became ill with the measles. While he was being treated, he was found to have progressive scleroderma, a rare disease that hardens the skin. In 1936 he spent much of the time in a great deal of pain and painted only 25 pictures.

PAINTING THROUGH ILLNESS

Between 1937 and 1939, Klee worked furiously, creating hundreds of paintings and 1,583 drawings. Despite his illness, he took part in the Bauhaus exhibition at the Museum of Modern Art in New York in 1938 and lent his work to numerous galleries in New York and Paris.

◀ Paul Klee in 1940 shortly before his death. In the years before his death, Klee's style of art changed. His pictures became bigger, less detailed and were filled with dark colours and strange symbols. Many of these symbols refer to death.

By 1939 Klee was getting weaker, the scleroderma made even the skin on his face hard. On 8 June 1940, Klee was rushed into hospital but his body was completely exhausted and he died on 29 June. Klee was cremated and his ashes later interred in Berne cemetry beside Lily's, on her death in 1946.

TIMELINE ▶

1935	1936	1937	1937	1939	1940	1946
Klee becomes ill. Progressive scleroderma is diagnosed.	Klee makes only 25 pictures.	The Nazis hold Degenerate Art Show. Klee's work is included.	The Nazis seize 102 of Klee's works from public museums. Klee's output increases hugely.	Germany invades Poland. World War II begins.	Klee dies on 29 June. Memorial exhibitions of his work are held in Berne and New York.	Paul and Lily Klee's ashes are interred in Berne, Switzerland.

Death and Fire, 1940
Tod und Feuer, 1940, 332

oil on canvas 46 x 44 cm Paul Klee Stiftung, Kunstmuseum, Berne, Switzerland

A ghostly skull stares out of this picture. The word 'Tod' appears twice – once in the face of the skull and once to the left of the skull (where the 'd' is formed by the skull itself). Tod is the German word for death. It is clear that Klee knew he was dying.

> *'Klee is ill, very ill... He needs the strength that remains to him for his work. That is all he lives for now.'*
>
> Rolf Bürgi, family friend, summer 1939

Klee's legacy

When Paul Klee died, the world was at war. Despite this people all over Europe and the United States mourned Klee's death. Memorial exhibitions of his work were held in Berne and in New York. His art is still admired and appreciated today and his writings continue to be important to artists and art historians.

CUBISM

Apart from his brief involvement with the Blue Riders (see pages 16-17), Klee did not belong to any of the important art movements of the time such as Cubism or Surrealism. However, his work still had an influence on both these styles of art. The way Klee drew everyday objects, emphasizing their most typical characteristics, was similar to the way the Cubists painted. Also, both the Cubists and Klee included words, signs and symbols in some of their pictures (see pages 24-5).

SURREALISM

The Surrealists painted pictures of fantastic worlds where clocks melt off tables and people have no faces. The Surrealists were inspired by the way Klee let his imagination run free when painting (see pages 20-21), by his inventions (see pages 26-7), and by the sense of humour in many of his pictures.

◀ *Breakfast*, Juan Gris, 1915.
Gris (1887-1927) was a Cubist painter and, like Klee, he featured everyday objects in his art, giving them meaning and importance.

'I cannot be grasped in the here and now
For my dwelling place is as much among the dead
As the yet unborn
Slightly closer to the heart of creation than usual
But still not close enough.'

The inscription on Paul Klee's tomb, originally from Paul Klee's diary

▲ *Alchemy*, Jackson Pollock, 1947. This picture was created by dripping, instead of brushing, paint onto the canvas.

KLEE'S INFLUENCE ON FUTURE ARTISTS

It was not just Klee's contemporaries that were inspired by his work. Jackson Pollock (1912-56) and Willem de Kooning (1904-97), the leading American Abstract Expressionist artists of the 1940s and 1950s, were interested in some of Klee's final works. In particular, they were attracted by the myths and symbols Klee invented, an area the Abstract Expressionists were obsessed with. Pollock and de Kooning were also influenced by the composition of Klee's last works, many of which have no central focus but force the viewer's eyes to travel on a journey around the whole picture, like Pollock's 'drip' paintings.

KLEE'S 'MAGIC'

Paul Klee's principal legacy is his art – it is incredibly beautiful and gives pleasure to people all over the world. At the time of his first successful show in 1917, art critics declared Paul Klee's work to be 'magical' and people still think so today. The magical aspect of Klee's art has a strong appeal for children and the new Paul Klee Centre in Berne includes a museum especially designed to encourage them in the creation of their own art.

◄ A model of the new home of the Paul Klee Centre in Berne which opened in 2005. The centre has a children's museum which aims to help develop skills for understanding and creating art using Klee's ideas on art techniques and theories. Klee thought the art of his childhood as important as his adult work, something the Paul Klee Centre has not forgotten.

Friends and colleagues

Paul Klee was friends with many artists and was influenced by their ideas, although he tried to keep his art uniquely his own. One of his longest relationships was with Wassily Kandinsky, whom he first met in 1911, when Kandinsky invited Klee to join the Blue Riders (see page 16). Klee was greatly impressed by the Russian artist and his new 'abstract' art.

> *His age of development was above mine. I could have been his pupil, and to a certain degree was...*
>
> *Paul Klee*

▲ When they first met, Klee recognised that Kandinsky had a clearer idea of where he wanted to take his art.

PARALLEL LIVES

Thereafter, Klee and Kandinsky shared similar lives: both became teachers and worked at the Bauhaus. When the school moved to Dessau in 1925 they even lived in two halves of the same house and shared a garden. And they both left Germany in 1933.

WASSILY KANDINSKY

Wassily Kandinsky was born in Russia in 1866. Inspired by Impressionist art, he left a career in the law and, in 1896, went to Munich to study painting. His early art was colourful and impressionistic, but around 1909 he began to take out its representational elements to create purely abstract art – his *Impressions* series (see page 16) was part of this process. After working with the Blue Riders, Kandinsky taught: in Russia from 1914–21 and at the Bauhaus (1922-33). He then went to France and lived outside Paris until his death in 1944.

TIMELINE ▶

1879	1901	1905	1907	1912	1916
18 December 1879 Paul Klee born, the second child of Hans and Ida.	**1901** Leaves the Academy. Engaged to Lily Stumpf.	**1905** Finishes the *Inventions*.	**30 November 1907** Lily and Paul's only child, Felix, is born.	**1912** Second Blue Rider Exhibition, Klee shows 17 pictures. Meets artist Robert Delaunay in Paris.	**1916** Marc killed. Klee conscripted. Works as a clerk.
1898 Travels to Munich. Studies at a private art school.	**October 1901** Travels to Italy.	**1905** Travels to Paris. Sees the work of the Impressionists.	**1908-1909** Sees art of Post-Impressionists.	**1913** Shows work at the *Galerie der Sturm* (The Storm Gallery).	**1917** Has a one-man exhibition at *Galerie der Sturm*.
1899 Meets his future wife, Lily Stumpf.	**May 1902** Returns to Berne, Switzerland.	**1905** Begins drawing his glass-pane pictures. Will produce 57 of them by 1912.	**1910** His first one-man show.	**1914** Goes to Tunisia. Paints in full colour for the first time. World War I begins. Macke is killed.	**11 November 1918** World War I ends. Germany is defeated.
1900 Gains a place at the Munich Academy of Art.	**1903** Starts working on the *Inventions*. The Wright brothers (USA) make the first powered flight.	**1906** His *Inventions* are exhibited. He and Lily get married.	**1911** Kandinsky founds The Blue Riders in Munich. Klee is invited to join the group.		**1919** Leaves the army. Gropius sets up the Bauhaus in Weimar.

SEPARATE IDEAS

As artists, they were often inspired by the same things – nature, music, the power of colour – yet the art they produced was very different. Unlike Kandinsky, Klee's art was never purely abstract.

Painting is a thunderous collision of differing worlds; a clash whose outcome is the creation of a new world which we call a work of art.

Wassily Kandinsky

▲ Kandinsky saw art as an almost violent process that created new worlds of understanding. Klee saw it as a more gentle process of revelation, showing the hidden nature of the world.

Once I worked at home all the time ... and then I suddenly discovered on a walk that actually nature is incredibly beautiful. I then tried to capture this. Now, too, I always make studies out of doors ... there is no area in which we can manage without nature studies.

Paul Klee

◀ Klee believed that painters should take their inspiration from nature and that pictures should always be partially recognizable, as this forced viewers to use their imagination.

Kandinsky thought that the best way ▶ for artists to reveal the world in paint was by creating 'absolute', or abstract, pictures (pictures without subjects) with 'pure' colour. It was the colour that triggered different emotions and moods.

A picture can be something other than a beautiful landscape, an interesting and picturesque scene, or the portrayal of a person.

Wassily Kandinsky

1920	1924	1930	1933	1935	1939
1920 Now famous. Has an exhibition of 326 pictures.	**1924** First exhibition in USA. The Bauhaus is closed in Weimar.	**1930** Exhibition at the Museum of Modern Art in New York.	**March 1933** Dessau flat searched by the Nazi authorities. His art is denounced.	**1935** Diagnosed with progressive scleroderma.	**1939** World War II begins.
1921 Begins teaching at the Bauhaus. Mother dies.	**1925** The Bauhaus opens in Dessau. First exhibition in Paris.	**1931** Resigns from the Bauhaus. Takes up a new teaching job at the Art Academy in Dusseldorf.	**April 1933** Sacked from job. The Nazis close down the Bauhaus.	**1936** Makes only 25 pictures.	**29 June 1940** Paul Klee dies. Memorial exhibitions of his work are held in Berne and New York.
1922 Kandinsky comes to the Bauhaus.	**1928** Travels to Egypt.			**1937** The Nazis hold Degenerate Art Show. Klee's work included. Nazis seize 102 of his works. Klee's output increases hugely.	**1945** World War II ends.
1923 Shows work in Bauhaus exhibition. Completes first 'magic square' pictures.	**1929** Exhibitions held in honour of his 50th birthday. New York stock market crashes. The Depression begins.		**30 January 1933** The Nazis in power. Hitler heads a coalition government.	**December 1933** The Klees move back to father's house in Berne, Switzerland.	**1946** Paul and Lily Klee's ashes are interred in Berne.

Glossary

abstract: art that does not imitate the world around us. It is usually impossible to recognise objects, people or places in abstract art.

Abstract Expressionism: the name given to the work of several artists painting in different but related ways in New York in the 1940s and 50s. Their work is abstract, its subject being the actual process of painting. Its most influential artists were Jackson Pollock (1912-56) and Willem de Kooning (1904-1997).

aesthetic: relating to a sense of beauty, particularly in art. Aesthetics is the study of the philosophy of art.

Aryan: in Nazi politics, a white person (called a Caucasian) descended from the original peoples of northern Europe.

avant-garde: describes new, experimental or radical ideas. From the French for vanguard, the first troops into battle.

concentration camp: a prison camp where civilians are held.

conscription: compulsory service in the armed forces.

Cubism: the name of an art movement evolving in Paris in about 1907 led by Pablo Picasso (1881-1973) and Georges Braque (1882-1963). The Cubists painted multiple angles of a person or object so they were all seen at once.

degenerate: something that has descended to a low moral, mental or aesthetic level.

etching: a print on paper made from an engraved metal plate.

Foundation year: The first year of art college, where students study several different areas of art.

Great Depression: the name given to the global economic slump of the 1930s.

Holocaust: the mass murder of the Jews of Europe by the Nazis between 1940 and 1945. Six million Jews were killed.

Impressionist: A group of artists based in Paris during the late nineteenth century who painted 'impressions' of the world with broad brushstrokes of pure, unmixed colour. The group included Auguste Renoir (1841-1919), Claude Monet (1840-1926) and Edgar Degas (1834-1917).

Nazi: anything to do with the National Socialist German Workers Party, the extreme right-wing political party lead by Adolf Hitler that ruled Germany between 1933 and 1945.

oil-transfer technique: a way of combining painting and drawing developed by Paul Klee where he would trace a drawing over an oil-covered sheet, pressing the oil, and so transferring the image, onto a pre-painted canvas underneath.

Old Masters: the name used to describe the greatest European painters from 1500-1800, including Leonardo da Vinci (1452-1519), Raphael (1483-1520), Michelangelo (1475-1564) and Caravaggio (1571-1610).

Orphism: an art movement that developed out of Cubism in the early twentieth century led by the French painter Robert Delaunay (1885-1941). Orphism allowed colour to dominate the picture, rather than form.

philosopher: someone who studies philosophy, the academic examination of scientific principles and human beliefs.

Post-Impressionist: a group of mostly French artists, although it included Dutchman Vincent van Gogh (1853-90), who were inspired and influenced by the Impressionists' use of pure colour.

propoganda: materials, such as publications, art and advertising, used by a government to get its policies across to the public.

scleroderma: a disease that causes skin to harden.

Surrealism: an art movement that emerged in the 1920s that tried to depict the life of our subconscious minds, or dreams. Its most famous artist is Salvador Dali (1904-1989).

tone: in art, the name for the combined effect of the colours and light and dark areas in a picture.

typography: the art of using type to set out a text. Used in publications, advertising and art.

watercolour: a painting created with colours (called pigments) diluted with water.

Museums and Galleries

Works by Klee are exhibited in museums and galleries all around the world. Some of the ones listed here are devoted solely to Klee, but most have a wide range of other artists' works on display.

   Even if you can't visit any of these galleries yourself, you may be able to visit their web sites. Gallery web sites often show pictures of the artworks they have on display. Some of the web sites even offer virtual tours which allow you to wander around and look at different paintings while sitting comfortably in front of your computer. Most of the international web sites listed below include an option that allows you to view them in English.

Bauhaus Museum of Design
Klingelhöferstrasse 14,
D-10785 Berlin,
Germany
www.bauhaus.de/english

Centre National d'Art et de Culture Georges Pompidou
75191 Paris
cedex 04,
France
www.centrepompidou.fr

Paul Klee Centre Foundation
Monument im Fruchtland 3
PO Box CH-3000
Berne 31
Switzerland
www.paulklee.ch

Paul Klee Stiftung
Kunstmuseum, Berne
Hodlerstrasse 12
3000 Berne 7
Switzerland
www.kunstmuseumbern.ch

Kunstbau Lenbachhaus
Lenbachhaus City Gallery
Luisenstrasse 33
80333 Munich
Germany
www.lenbachhaus.de

Kunstmuseum, Basle
St. Alban-Graben 16,
CH-4010 Basle,
Germany
www.kunstmuseumbasel.ch

Museum Ludwig
Bischofsgartenstrasse 1,
D - 50667 Köln,
Germany
www.museenkoeln.de/ludwig

The Museum of Modern Art
11 West 53 Street
New York,
NY 10019-5497
USA
www.moma.org

National Gallery of Australia
Parkes Place, Canberra
ACT 2601
www.nga.gov.au

Sprengel Museum
Kurt-Schwitters-Platz
30169 Hanover
Germany
www.sprengel-museum.de

Tate Modern
Bankside
London SE1 9TG
www.tate.org.uk/modern

Index